INTRODUCTION

■ The Changing Nature of Venture Capital

The venture capital industry has reached middle age. After years of growth in the amount of money raised and invested, the number of transactions completed, and the number of players in the market, the mid-1990s has witnessed the levelling out of transactions and the first signs of rationalisation in the market. The number of financiers has begun to shrink.

Venture capital, once the domain of both little and big players, has increasingly become dominated by the large institutions – banks, insurance companies and pension funds – working through specialist business units or subsidiaries. Only the very successful independent firms have been able to raise new funds in the tough fund-raising conditions following the recession of the early 1990s, when business failures made weaknesses in portfolios apparent to the scrutinising fund investor.

As fund-raising has generally followed stock market cycles, with peak fund-raising following successful flotation of investee companies, many venture capitalists who didn't profit from the strong stock market in 1994 and 1995 by raising new funds are no longer in business.

Those which still are increasingly focus on less risky investments: buy-outs and development capital. Only the big or the bold still dabble in what was originally meant by 'venture capital' – finance for creating new companies.

Now, more often than not, the only new companies venture capitalists finance are simply the holding companies set up to buy an existing business in the typical management buy-out structure. New *business* finance has been left to a small number of players.

■ Definitions

'Venture capital' is now usually taken to refer to any investment in private, unlisted companies. The new names reflect this: 'Midland Montagu Ventures' became 'Montagu Private Equity', after Midland Bank was taken over by Hong Kong & Shanghai Banking Corporation; when Royal Bank of Scotland decided to enter the business, it was 'development', not 'venture' that described their business unit.

In fact, so much of the so-called venture capital investment has been directed to established or mature businesses, it is correct to understand true venture capital – investing in start-up and early-stage companies – to represent only a minor subset of the total industry.

MARKET AND INDUSTRY

The following statistics of the UK venture capital market substantiate this claim.

UK START-UP AND EARLY-STAGE FUNDING

Year	Number of transactions		Value (£m)	
	Start-up	Early stage	Start-up	Early stage
1986	166	108	58	28
1987	267	191	75	45
1988	202	182	70	60
1989	177	344	86	129
1990	199	141	76	52
1991	158	115	35	23
1992	130	92	43	39
1993	123	113	34	35
1994	100	77	45	31

Source: British Venture Capital Association

About half of the £76m of venture capital for start-up and early-stage companies in 1994 was provided by 3i, the UK's largest venture capitalist. The other half came from a handful of other firms, some who balance start-up investment with buy-out and later-stage development financing.

In Continental Europe, a similar situation exists, with an estimated ECU300m invested throughout Europe in start-up and early stage companies in 1994. Much of this money comes from government-sponsored funds, often targeted for areas of high unemployment to encourage the creation of new industries and jobs.

While regional grants and aid are available in the UK, this source of funding does not play as significant role as it does elsewhere in Europe. The Conservative UK Government has limited the use of direct government-funding of new companies, favouring tax incentives for the private sector instead. Tax incentives, such as the Business Expansion Scheme (BES) which ran from 1988–94 and the Venture Capital Trusts which replaced it in 1994, have helped promote investment into early stage venture capital investment.

One of the reasons the BES scheme was disbanded, however, was criticism that it served more as a tax-avoidance device than providing real incentive to invest in risky ventures.

While the absolute investment amount in early stage financings is small, the number of transactions – about 200 in each of the past three years – is still considerable. The average start-up deal size is under £500,000 – only a tenth the size of the average buy-out investment. As most venture capitalists will attest, the £500,000 early-stage investment will, more often than not, take just as long to negotiate, structure and monitor, as the £5,000,000 buy-out deal. The early-stage investment will therefore need to achieve a significantly higher rate of return than the buy-out, in order for the investor to make anything near the absolute return he would achieve on the buy-out.

CONTENTS

WELCOME

*Welcome to this self-study workbook on **Venture Capital**, which aims to provide a basic understanding of the current venture capital market in the UK and Europe and how venture capital investments are structured. Because buy-outs have become the principal part of the venture capitalists' business, valuing and structuring leveraged transactions is also considered. The different types of capital that fund buy-outs is likewise discussed.*

Read each section carefully and test your understanding as you go along by completing the exercises. Please note that there may be more than one correct answer to certain questions. You can check your progress against the answers on page 29.

When you have completed this workbook, you should have achieved a thorough understanding of the venture capital business.

FOREWORD

After leaving my employment as a corporate financier with Bankers Trust I have been involved in the training of bankers in many parts of the world for over a decade. The company I set up in 1984 now trades as DC Gardner/Euromoney and continues to provide training in many aspects of banking. Although no longer involved with the company that bears my name, I continue to be fascinated by the field of professional training and education for bankers, and through my association with Fairplace, I am able to maintain an active participation in this area.

The world of banking has changed considerably during the past ten years: financial instruments have become much more complex, risks have become ever more difficult to identify, let alone to manage and control, and ever advancing technology continues to change the ways in which banks operate.

As the structures, products and services, risks and technology of banks have changed, so too has the development of people. A new era in banking is now upon us, where familiarity with yesterday's skills will no longer be valued. Tomorrow's bank employees will be more 'knowledge workers' than information processors. For me, this means exciting new training and development opportunities to explore. Not only in terms of the contents of training but also through different delivery systems.

There is no doubt that multi-media training materials will prove to be effective delivery tools, but I firmly believe that both classroom-based and paper-based training will continue to be in strong demand. Consequently, it has been a great pleasure to be involved in the production of this series of training workbooks. The texts have been produced by the faculty of trainers and consultants at Fairplace,

who have been selected for their excellent skills both as practitioners and communicators. I am confident if you read the books carefully and attempt the exercises diligently you will gain much from these workbooks, and in so doing you will be adding to your employability in this volatile new world of banking.

Colyn Gardner

Dr DC Gardner
Cornhill
The City of London

That is why so many venture capitalists have turned their attention to later-stage development capital financings and the larger buy-outs, where returns can be higher, and risks arguably lower.

BUY-OUT MARKET

UK market statistics*

Year	Number of transactions	Value** (£m)	Average size (m)
1986	300	1300	4.3
1987	350	3230	9.2
1988	400	5070	12.7
1989	500	6530	13.1
1990	550	2860	5.2
1991	500	2640	5.3
1992	520	3020	5.8
1993	510	2810	5.5
1994	550	3570	6.5
1995	600	4660	7.8

* taken from KPMG-'Management Buy-out Statistics'

** Represents value of total transaction, i.e., all forms of capital used

The total number of buy-outs completed each year in Europe is estimated to roughly equal the number in the UK. Considerable commentary has been made as to why buy-out finance has taken hold in the UK to such a greater degree than in other European countries.

The principal reasons are summarised as follows:

Legal

The UK is more 'lender-friendly' than other legal jurisdictions. This has encouraged the development of the senior debt market and leveraged capital structures which augments returns to the equity providers.

Cultural

UK managers are more profit-oriented than their Continental counterparts. There is a much stronger sense that the sole or principal obligation of companies is to provide profits for shareholders, including management.

In many European countries, companies are seen to be acting as much for employees and the communities in which they reside as for shareholders. The link between corporate ownership and shareholder value is much weaker. Managers are less concerned about becoming rich than they are about their position in society. Employees have much greater authority in influencing corporate decisions and have greater ability in protecting their own rights through trade unions.

Capital Markets

A large and active stock market is crucial to the buy-out industry, as the stock market is one of the main exit routes for buy-out investors. Because the London Stock Exchange is one of the three largest stock markets in the world, it follows that the buy-out market also benefits. The development of the British buy-out market resembles in many respects the US market, in which many of the legal, cultural and social characteristics are common to both countries.

■ Financiers

Equity Investors

It is estimated that there are about 80 equity investors who consistently compete in the European buy-out market. These players include all of the independent funds and in-house venture capital units of the large banks and financial institutions (pension fund managers like CIN or insurance companies like PruVentures, a subsidiary of Prudential Assurance) and the banks providing senior debt.

Independent firms raised a record £2.6bn of new funds for investment in the equity of buy-out transactions in 1995, a record amount, breaching the previous peak year of 1989, and a significant increase over the the 1994 figure of £479m.

It is estimated that the amount of funds managed by the independent firms is matched by the amount made available by the in-house subsidiaries of banks, giving a total of over £5bn of equity available for investment in 1995.

Given that buy-out transactions currently are funded with roughly equal amounts of debt and equity, the total available capital would support a market size of some £10bn, about two years' market at the 1995 market size.

It is clear from these statistics that there is a surplus of capital available to meet the current level of demand, prompting market players to complain that there is too much capital chasing too few good deals. As in any supply and demand equation, this means that there is upward pressure on prices being paid for companies, the result of which will likely lead to lower returns when the current round of investments are realised during the next three-five years (the typical period before buy-out investors are able to realise ('exit') their investments through stock market flotation or trade sale).

Senior Debt Providers

There are between 45–50 banks which compete in the European buy-out market. Virtually every bank which has a presence in the market maintains a London presence, even if its head office is in Continental Europe. All large European transactions are syndicated out of London.

While there are many banks competing in the market, the five major UK clearing banks have continued to dominate the market, providing the senior debt in between 70–80% of all transactions during the mid-1990s. The two market leaders, NatWest and Bank of Scotland, together provide between 40–45%, with the other three – Royal Bank of Scotland, Barclays and Midland

– providing the rest. Lloyds Bank is the only UK clearer not to have a significant presence in the buy-out market.

There is a second tier of some 10–15 banks which have the ability to underwrite significant amounts of debt for the larger buy-outs. These banks include the large Continental banks: UBS, Société Generale, Banque Indosuez; US banks: Bankers Trust, Chemical, Bank of America; and some of the larger merchant banks, including Deutsche Morgan Grenfell and Hambros.

Following the second tier are another 30 or so banks which actively participate in the larger syndicated loans. By 1995, the Japanese banks, who were out of the market during the recessionary years, were beginning to seek both underwriting roles and participations in the senior debt of buy-outs.

There are several trends which have emerged in the senior debt market since the recession. First, is the overall level of competition for both lead arranger/underwriting mandates as well as for participations in syndicated deals. Underwriting limits have increased. At the depth of the recession in 1991–92, there were few banks willing to underwrite even £25m of senior debt. By 1994 there were at least 12 banks actively seeking opportunities to underwrite as much as twice that amount.

Likewise arrangers are looking for participants who are willing to take and hold much larger amounts. Some of the larger deals completed in 1995 were syndicated on a minimum take level of £15m and most required commitments of at least £10m. The push for higher hold levels results both from arrangers' desire to reduce their own work in forming syndicates, and memories of the work-out years during the recession, when large unwieldy bank groups made restructurings extremely difficult and time-consuming.

There is also an element of reciprocity that drives the formation of syndicates, as most of the arrangers are also looking for participations. Inviting other large banks into their own deals, arrangers create opportunities for themselves. One of the characteristics of a mature market is not only increased competition amongst the lead players, but also consolidation of groups when appropriate. This is most apparent when investor groups, backed by a senior lender group, are bidding in competition for a buy-out mandate. The losing group has often conducted significant due diligence and is therefore in a good position to be able to commit to a transaction quickly. This also makes the syndication job easier for the arranger of the winning group.

Mezzanine providers

The third section of the buy-out market is the mezzanine providers. Mezzanine, the capital which ranks between senior debt and equity in the capital structure in many buy-outs, is a much smaller component than the other two. There are therefore far fewer players.

There are only four independent mezzanine funds or companies, including Intermediate Capital Group plc, by far the largest, Mezzanine Management Limited, who manage the First Britannia Fund, Mithras Trust plc, the listed entity managed by Legal and General Ventures, and the Kleinwort mezzanine fund, managed by the merchant bank.

There are also many banks willing to provide mezzanine in buy-outs. The smaller banks manage the activity within their senior debt lending groups; the larger banks, like NatWest, have separate mezzanine units, in order to remove any potential conflict of interest between the interests of the two types of lender.

Exercise 1

1. What are the principal reasons why the UK buy-out market is larger than any one Continental European country market?

2. What are the principal sources of start-up and early stage venture capital?

3. Why do venture capitalists prefer to invest in buy-outs?

TYPES OF INVESTMENT

■ Early-stage Investments

Start-up or 'greenfield' investments include a broad range of businesses. Start-ups include investment for new product development, such as new drugs developed through biotechnology, or software or other computer-related products.

Start-ups can also involve transferring a successful business concept from one country to another. Start-up finance is required for establishing manufacturing plant and administrative offices for the new companies. This type of venture finance is often provided as part of a joint venture with an industrial partner. The best examples of joint venture start-ups are found in emerging markets – eastern Europe and the former Soviet states, certain countries in the Far East such as Thailand and Singapore, and Latin America. Because the established markets of the US and Europe are mature and more competitive, many successful venture capitalists are venturing further afield in seeking high growth rates.

The early-stage investment is aimed at achieving excellent rates of return through equally rapid rates of growth in corporate value. With the exception of some joint ventures with strong corporate partners, most early stage investments represent much higher than normal business risks. As start-up companies with no proven cash flow, the new company cannot be expected to service debt. For this reason, start-up ventures are funded almost entirely with equity. In order for the equity investor to achieve returns commensurate with the high business risks assumed in a new venture, growth of the company must be exceptional.

The most spectacular examples of start-up investment successes are the computer companies of the early to mid-1980s, including such names as Lotus, Microsoft and Compaq.

Usually start-up companies need two or three rounds of equity finance before the company is ready to take on any debt. Depending on the nature of the business – whether it is a manufacturer requiring significant levels of working capital (inventory and receivables) and whether it is earning high profit margins – will determine the level of debt the business needs or can support. Software companies, for example, not only tend to earn high operating margins (product uniqueness commands higher prices and profits) but also do not require as much working capital finance as a manufacturer. This means that venture-funding can often take them through to a later stage of development without significant levels of debt. Stock market flotation is possible based on proven initial products. Flotation proceeds enable the company to fund the development of new products and can also be distributed to the initial venture capital financiers.

■ Development Capital

Development capital, as distinct from start-up or early-stage funding, is precisely the providing of finance for secondary stages of corporate development. Investors providing development capital look for companies which have: *proven products* – technologically proven as well as accepted in the market; *experienced management teams* – many inventive founders are not capable of taking the company to the next stage of development. Helping a company identify and hire executives experienced in putting into place appropriate organisation structures is very much part of the venture capitalist's job, but founders must have the willingness and appreciation of the importance of needing to change the organisation to fit a new stage of development.

Investing in developing companies is usually not as risky as investing in start-ups, but the activity carries its own dynamic. Here the successful venture capitalist 'brings more to the table' than just his wallet. He needs to have an understanding of how developing companies should be managed. This usually means having had direct experience of managing a similar company himself. Many venture capital firms will only hire executives with managerial experience. However, it has also been made apparent that the experience must be of the right kind. Experienced managers of large mature companies are not necessarily the best people to be advising young growing companies. A careful balance must be struck between imposing corporate structures and encouraging creativity and flexibility.

■ Buy-outs

While buy-outs are not new to corporate finance, as retiring owners of businesses have always had the option of selling their companies to the remaining management team, the buy-out phenomenon in the western world did not begin in earnest until the early 1980s – less than two decades ago.

Despite the general awareness of buy-outs and associated terminology, the exact definition of a buy-out is not widely understood outside the financial world. A buy-out is defined as any corporate acquisition in which the assets and cash flow of the company being bought are used to finance the transaction. A buy-out is therefore distinct from a normal corporate acquisition in which the purchasing company raises finance based on its own financial status.

Types of Buy-outs

A 'management buy-out' (or MBO) is one in which the existing managers of the target acquire a controlling or significant shareholding in the company through the transaction. If the company being bought is small, management may be able to achieve a large stake and control the direction of the transaction.

If the business being bought is large, then management may have little or no role in the negotiation of the transaction. In fact, with the significant competition characteristic of the market in the mid-1990s, management

teams are sometimes not consulted at all in the bidding process. Competing buy-out firms may be bidding against each other and negotiating directly with the vendor. Buy-out firms may be acting just like corporate acquirers, taking responsibility for making up for any deficiencies in the existing management team after the company is bought.

A management 'buy-in' is one in which the existing management team is being replaced by newcomers. This occurs when managers are owners and are selling to a new management team, where the existing management team is known or believed to be inadequate, or when buy-out firms are competing against each other and one has the backing of the existing management team.

One variation of the buy-in is the inelegantly named BIMBO ('buy-in management buy-out') in which the existing management team is supplemented by new executives.

Leveraged buy-outs (LBOs) refer to a buy-out in which a significant amount or degree of debt is used to purchase the company. In some ways, the buy-out phenomenon really got started with the availability of leverage. Because the buy-out market took off during a period of strong economic growth, where earnings increases could be assumed, leveraging transactions was readily achievable. Most buy-outs were leveraged and the terms 'buy-out' and 'leveraged buy-out' were synonymous.

Following the recession, in which buy-out failures became legendary, much more conservative capital structures were employed. Leveraged structures normally meant at least 60% debt, but up to 90% (including all forms of debt), in the capital structure.

In 1989 the US banking regulators – the Federal Reserve Board, the Office of the Controller of the Currency, and the Federal Deposit Insurance Corporation – jointly adopted the definition of a 'highly leveraged transaction' ('HLT') as any corporate financing transaction which either:

■ doubles a company's liabilities and results in a leverage ratio (total liabilities divided by total assets, including intangibles) greater than 50%; *or*

■ results in a leverage ratio greater than 75%.

While the US authorities stopped requiring banks to report the amount of their HLT portfolios in 1993, many US banks and some European banks still report the size of their HLT exposure and/or use the definition to monitor and limit their exposure to financial leverage.

While buy-outs introduce ownership change, a company can undergo a transformation of its capital structure without changing ownership. A 'recapitalisation' or 'recap' refers to a transaction in which a company replaces its equity capital with debt. This can be accomplished in several ways:

1 through a significant special dividend paid to existing shareholders funded through a bank loan or by issuing debt securities. This enables the shareholders to maintain their pro rata ownership while realising part of their investment in a company;

2 through an offer to purchase shares back from shareholders (again through borrowed money). This enables certain shareholders to sell out completely and others to increase their stake;

3 by setting up a new company and offering to purchase all of the outstanding shares of the target company. This legal structure is essentially the same as used in a leveraged buy-out and would be used in a recap if a public company were being taken private.

Because companies undergoing buy-outs can range from smaller family-run companies facing ownership transition problems to large divisions of multinational corporations, the investor likewise has a range of corporate issues to consider.

Normally, buy-out investors are looking for mature companies with proven cash flow. Buy-outs are conceived and expected to involve only one investment transaction. Follow-on investment is only needed if financial performance after the buy-out falls significantly below expectations.

The degree to which buy-outs can be leveraged depends on the stage of development the target company is in. Mature companies with proven cash flows – businesses presenting low business risks – can be more highly leveraged. Companies still in early stages of development – which are growing rapidly and consuming cash or are not yet proven businesses – can support less debt.

Characteristics of the Ideal Candidate for an LBO

The ideal candidate for the leveraged buy-out has the following characteristics:

Strong Market Share

The company should have a dominant position in its market or market niche. This tends to mean that the company understands and has successfully reacted to market dynamics. There may be strong barriers to entry into the market – financial, relationship, or product patents, etc.

Mature Company in a Mature Market

With a well-established competitive position, the market itself should be mature. This means slow overall growth and few radical changes. Competitive patterns and market development should be predictable.

Long Product Cycle

The company's products should not be subject to rapid technological change. With a long product cycle, significant ongoing R&D expenditure should not be necessary.

No Change in Business Strategy

The company's continuing success should not require a significant change in strategy. The company's business plan should read 'continue to do the same old thing'.

No Rationalisation

The company should not require overhaul of its overhead base or substantial cost-cutting to make it sufficiently profitable to service the proposed level of debt. In many buy-outs there are opportunities to cut costs, but the future success of the business should not depend on it. It is often the case that new management can spot opportunities to make cost reductions that an existing management team does not. This is often one of the benefits of the management buy-in, where a new team replaces or augments existing senior management.

Experienced Management

New management itself, however, poses an additional risk as it does not have the experience of the existing management team and may well make some mistakes as it learns about the company. Generally it is less risky investing in a company in which the management team does not have to be changed – assuming of course, that the existing team is up to scratch.

Generating a strong predictable cash flow to service debt is the overall objective of the company which has undergone a leveraged buy-out. The characteristics of the ideal candidate all contribute to this objective.

A company with a *strong market share* should not need to spend significant sums of money establishing itself in the market. Its brand names, etc. should have already been established. *Long product cycles* mean the company is not spending large sums of money on R&D or capital equipment. Buy-out candidates do not require substantial investment in fixed assets, nor have they just finished the peak of their expenditure cycle before being bought out. *Mature companies* grow slowly if at all. This means investment in working capital – inventory and receivables – is not substantial. So the degree to which a company's earnings and cash flow is strong and predictable is the degree to which it can be leveraged.

■ Turnarounds

Many companies which have gone bankrupt still have a viable future. While the reasons for bankruptcy are various, many times corrective action can be taken and the company can be turned around. This is where the venture capitalist comes in.

Some of the best investments have been in companies which are being sold by an administrator, receiver or bankruptcy court. Companies which are in bankruptcy tend to be sold cheaply. There is often a further 'price reduction' that can be achieved through negotiations with creditors. Suppliers to the company are usually willing to take discounts on the amounts they are owed, in order to help the company emerge from bankruptcy so that some recovery of the debt can be achieved over time. If alternative sources of supplies are available, then the company may not need to pay back any of the pre-bankruptcy debt. Because most companies take debtor insurance on financially-weak customers, they can also afford to make compromises in collecting their debts.

Bankrupt companies usually afford some lessons to the incoming investors. If the reasons for the bankruptcy are understood and actions have or can be taken to correct the mistakes, then buying companies out of bankruptcy can make sense.

As with start-up and early-stage companies, the company emerging from bankruptcy should not normally be highly leveraged. Given that over-leverage was the main reason companies went bankrupt during the recession, one of the basic lessons of bankruptcy is that leverage accentuates any strategic mistakes that have been made. While every bankruptcy can, in some sense, be said to have resulted from poor management decisions, these errors can be overcome if the company has sufficient financial flexibility. There are certainly many examples of financially strong companies having made extremely poor business decisions but surviving because they had the financial resources to correct their mistakes.

In deciding whether to invest in a bankrupt company, the venture capitalist must first of all identify exactly what went wrong and what has or can be done about it. Purchasing a company out of bankruptcy cannot simply be 'business as usual.' The venture capitalist must often replace key executives and even assume an executive role for some period of time himself. He must ensure that any tarnished reputation is overcome and must re-establish or create new relationships with customers and suppliers.

Investing in turnarounds presents its own set of risks and work, but companies which have gone bust at least have some track record which can assist investment decisions. This is more than can be said of start-ups, which have no track record.

Exercise 2

1. What are the principal characteristics of a company which can withstand a high degree of leverage?

2. Which statement(s) describes a buy-out?

    a) A corporate acquisition in which the existing management team takes a controlling ownership stake or plays an important role in the transaction.

    b) An acquisition in which the assets and cash flow of the target company are used to support the transaction.

    c) A transaction in which a significant amount or proportion of debt is used in the capital structure.

    d) An acquisition in which new management team is introduced to a company.

3. Why should start-up or early stage companies generally not be highly leveraged?

TYPES OF CAPITAL

Module 4

■ Definitions

There are many types of debt and equity instruments used in venture capital investment, depending on the type of investment being made and the overall objective of the transaction.

Given the wide variety of instruments available and the various hybrids that can be formed, the distinction between debt and equity is often blurred. The most straightforward approach to determining what is debt and what is equity is to consider regulatory, accounting, and tax treatments. Any form of capital which imposes an obligation on a company to make specified payments at specified times is generally considered by regulatory authorities as debt (even if is labelled 'capital' or similar non-debt sounding name). Accountancy practice follows the same principle.

From a corporate finance standpoint, tax treatment is more important. Any form of capital in which payments to the supplier of the capital are deductible against taxable profits is by definition debt. This fundamental principle – that interest expense is tax-deductible whereas dividends are not – prevails in most jurisdictions in the world.

■ Debt Instruments

Senior Debt

The simplest form of debt is bank borrowings. Banks are the normal source and provide the bulk of debt finance for buy-outs and to the degree possible, early-stage corporate financings.

Banks will normally only provide working capital finance for early stage companies. This can take the form of factoring or invoice discounting, in which the credit quality of the debtor is as important as the credit strength of the borrower. This type of facility enables the early-stage company to fund some of the growth of the working capital, as availability of credit is directly tied to the level of debtors. High-growth companies with a good quality customer base can therefore obtain some support for working capital growth.

Working capital finance in whatever form, is always short-term. This means that the lender is not committed to continue to lend for any particular period. The loan is 'on demand' and can be recalled whenever the lender wishes.

In buy-out transactions involving a target company with strong and stable cash flow, longer term bank debt is justifiable. The normal repayment period for 'term loans' made available as part of the finance for buy-outs and acquisitions is between five to seven years.

The other principal terms and conditions for bank loans used in buy-outs are as follows:

1. Security
Bank loans are usually always secured on all of the assets of the target company.

2. Priority
The bank's claim on the assets and cash flow of the target company takes priority over any other lender's claim. This is the meaning of 'senior debt'.

3. Covenants
A term loan always has covenants which track the company's performance after the transaction. Financial covenants specify the benchmarks against which the bank is willing to lend and are usually based on the lender's best estimate of what he thinks will happen. This may or may not differ from the financial projections provided by the management buy-out team. Financial covenants should be meaningful – viz., they should be triggered well before

the company has a problem with making interest or principal payments, but not so tight as to be triggered for only slight underperformance to plan.

The principal covenants that buy-out lenders use are:

1. Interest coverage tests

Measured as operating earnings (Earnings before interest and tax, or 'EBIT' divided by senior or sometimes, total interest expense). Interest coverage is also tested on a cash flow basis; some lenders will argue that the EBIT/interest test provides only an approximation of a company's ability to service interest, as it ignores taxes and required investment in fixed assets and working capital. A better interest cover test measures cash flow (defined as EBITDA less capital expenditure and cash taxes; or 'free cash flow', which also deducts working capital investment)divided by interest expense.

2. Net worth and leverage tests

A net-worth test measures the expected increase in balance sheet value of a company and is not particularly useful on its own. Leverage tests compare total borrowings or total liabilities to net worth, and are therefore more useful as an overall indication of financial strength and stability.

Other covenants test a company's liquidity and working capital efficiency, and are used in situations where management of these items is critical to the health of the company.

Pricing

Senior lenders in the European market of the mid-1990s expect to earn a margin of between 1.5%–2.5% over their cost of funds. In the US, margins average .5%–1.0% higher. Senior lenders charge up-front fees of between 1%–2% of the principal amount of the loan.

■ Subordinated Debt

Subordinated debt ranks after senior debt in its claim on the assets and cash flow of the borrower. It can take many forms. In buy-outs, 'mezzanine' debt is provided by a handful of specialists who will normally mirror the covenants and security arrangements of the senior debt agreement. In addition to a margin on his cost of funds, and a fee, the mezzanine lender expects an enhanced return by way of warrants or options to purchase shares in a company. Mezzanine lenders expect to achieve Internal Rates of Return (IRR) between 15–20% in the low stable interest rate environment of the mid-1990s.

In the 1980s, subordinated debt was also readily available in the form of tradeable securities. They were known as 'high-yield bonds' and earned the label of 'junk bonds' once the incidence of default became apparent. High yield bonds are much less part of the buy-out scene in the 1990s.

They have been replaced to some extent by more exotic forms of senior debt. Bankers Trust has pioneered the use of 'B loans' which are *pari passu* with senior debt in every respect except repayment schedule. The B loan providers, mostly insurance companies looking to match long-term insurance policy premia receipts with long-term investments, provide the 'back end' of a senior loan repayment schedule. In a typical seven-year term loan, the banks will be repaid during years 1–5 and the B loan provider will be repaid in years 6 and 7. Another form of debt becoming increasingly popular in the US is convertible debt. Various versions of both senior and subordinated debt are available for buy-out finance. The characteristics common to all forms are that they are secured and convertible into common share capital at some predetermined price or formula.

■ Equity

Like debt instruments, equity capital can come in many different forms. Ordinary (or common) shares represent the fundamental ownership and economic interest in a company. Unlike all other forms of capital, ordinary shares have the greatest variation in ultimate value. Ordinary shareholders have the most to gain in the success of any business venture.

The most significant, and often the most difficult, negotiation that occurs between the venture capitalist and the management team is entitlement to the ordinary equity of the company. The venture capitalist seeks an ownership stake sufficient to enable him to achieve his targeted return on the investment.

In buy-out transactions of the mid-1990s, this usually ranges between 20–30%. In start-ups and early stage investments, the targeted IRR rises to a minimum of 30% (with some investments expected to achieve returns well in excess of this).

Venture capitalists will also provide preference (preferred) shares or sometimes subordinated debt alongside ordinary share capital. This enables him to structure the agreed ownership split between managers and equity investors while still providing the required amount of equity capital for the venture. Preference shares provide the cushion for the lenders – it is part of the risk capital being provided by the venture capitalist – but does not dilute the managers' shareholding as preference shares have no voting rights or variable claim on the economic value of the enterprise.

Preference shares may or may not have a fixed dividend, depending on the strength of the cash flow and the interest rate environment. (If interest rates are high, much of the company's cash flow will go to pay the lenders' interest). The extent to which cash flow is adequate to pay preference share dividends will limit the proportion of ordinary shares required by the investor.

Example

A venture capitalist is making an investment in an early stage company and aims to achieve an IRR of 30%. Because the company's cash flow is weak in the initial years of the investment, the venture capitalist structures his investment in the form of preference shares which pay a fixed dividend of 6% and ordinary shares which pay no dividend but partake of the ultimate economic value of the firm. The investment required is £1.1m: £1.0m in the form of preference shares and £0.1m in the form of ordinary shares. The ordinary equity of the company is projected to be worth £10.0m in five years' time. In order to achieve his targeted IRR he would need to be entitled to a 26% stake in the ordinary shares. Assuming no other equity holders, the management team would be entitled to the remaining 74% shareholding.

The cash flow on the venture capitalist's investment is as follows:

(£000)	Day 1	Yr. 1	Yr. 2	Yr. 3	Yr. 4	Yr. 5
Investment	(1100)	–	–	–	–	–
Pref. dividend	–	60	60	60	60	60
Pref. repayment	–	–	–	–	–	1000
Ordinary share value	–	–	–	–	–	2600
Totals	(1100)	60	60	60	60	3660
IRR=30.4%						

Now suppose that the cash flow of the company is sufficiently strong to enable the company to pay a preference share dividend of 12% per annum. With all other assumptions the same, the investor will need only a 20% stake in order to achieve his targeted IRR of 30%:

(£000)	Day 1	Yr. 1	Yr. 2	Yr. 3	Yr. 4	Yr. 5
Investment	(1100)	–	–	–	–	–
Pref. dividend	–	120	120	120	120	120
Pref. repayment	–	–	–	–	–	1000
Ordinary share value	–	–	–	–	–	2000
Totals	(1100)	120	120	120	120	3120
IRR=30.01%						

Only a modest difference in the dividend payable leaves an additional 6% of the equity in the hands of the managers, which is worth £600,000 in five years' time.

Exercise 3

1. What are the principal characteristics of senior debt used in buy-outs?

2. Which of the following statements are not true?

a) Mezzanine debt can share many of the features of senior debt.

b) Mezzanine debt is often secured.

c) Venture capitalists providing ordinary or common share capital would generally not provide preference share capital as well.

d) During periods of low inflation and interest rates, buy-out investors seek higher returns (IRRs).

e) Venture capitalists generally seek higher returns from investing in early-stage companies than from investing in buy-outs.

3. Why should equity investors be entitled to the highest returns amongst the providers of capital for buy-outs?

STRUCTURING THE TRANSACTION

■ Valuing the Target

The starting point of any venture capital investment decision is valuing the investee company. This is required in order for the investor to calculate his required rate of return.

The investor approaches the valuation exercise by asking himself what he thinks the company will be worth at some point in the future – the point at which the company could be sold or floated on a stock exchange so that the investor could realise all or part of his investment. The value of the company at this point in the future is referred to as the 'terminal value', 'continuing value' or 'exit value'.

The reason why terminal values are more important in venture capital investing is that the company may not have any obvious present value. Determining what the value of the company may be in the future may also be difficult, but the exercise at least focuses thought and analysis on the principal components of value and how value will be created.

Every venture investment begins with a business plan and financial forecast. Analysing the forecasts is usually conducted after an initial study of the basic business concept and strategy, including an assessment of the management team. Assuming the proposal passes this first step, the venture capitalist then needs to judge whether the financial forecasts are coherent, and consistent with the strategy.

While the venture capitalist may change some of the assumptions, perform his own sensitivity analysis on the numbers, and even help the managers prepare the plan, it is important that the managers themselves take responsibility for preparing the forecast and understanding the implications. Without a high level of commitment to the financial plan, the chances of success will not be as good.

■ Deriving Terminal Values

Terminal values are calculated in two ways: as a multiple of earnings for the specified future year, or as the sum of all future cash flows (present-valued at the terminal value date). Probably because venture capital investors often think of flotation as a possible or likely 'exit route', using price/earnings ratios (multiples) to derive terminal values is the more usual method. It is also considerably easier.

Price earnings (or P/E) ratios are reported in virtually every publication which analyses corporate performance, including the financial press and many daily newspapers.

P/E ratios are calculated as either:

- A company's *share price* divided by its *earnings per share* (EPS); or,

- The company's total market capitalisation (total shares outstanding multiplied by price per share), divided by total *net earnings* (earnings or profits after all financing costs, taxes and any extraordinary or exceptional items, but before dividend payments).

There is a considerable amount of information on P/E ratios. Ample historical stock market and sectoral data is available enabling the analyst to make meaningful comparisons between companies. If, for example, the company being valued operates in an industry in which the average P/E is 16.5×, then it would be reasonable to calculate the terminal value of the company as 16.5 times the earnings projected for the terminal year.

P/E multiples incorporate the market's expectation of future earnings growth, reflecting both an individual company's past and expected future performance and the growth dynamic of the industry sector.

Having estimated a terminal value, the venture capitalist can then determine how much of that terminal value he will need in order to achieve his required rate of return. The proportion of the terminal value required will determine the percentage ownership (of the ordinary or common share capital) that the investor will want. Because the venture capitalist will also have analysed the business plan and forecast, he will already know how much finance is required for the project. If he assumes that he will provide all of the required finance in the form of equity, which would be usual for a start-up, the cash flow calculation is straightforward. He may also need to factor in the possibility of second and third-round equity financings which will, of course, lower his IRR.

Example

A venture capital investor is considering investing $5m in a new medical supply company. The average P/E for the industry is 22.3×, above the overall market average, reflecting the higher growth prospects of the business. The investor expects to float the company in the fifth year after his investment, on the back of the results for the fourth year. He believes the company will achieve net earnings of $3.5m in year 4, and calculates a terminal value of $78.05m (= 22.3 × $3.5m), which is the value he believes he would achieve on a flotation of the company in year 5.

Assuming he receives no dividends over the five-year period, the investor would achieve an IRR of 36.2% on the basis of a 30% shareholding in the firm.

The cash flow portrayal is as follows:

($000)	Day 1	Yr. 1	Yr. 2	Yr. 3	Yr. 4	Yr. 5
Investment	(5000)	–	–	–	–	–
Investment value	–	–	–	–	–	23,420
Totals	(5000)	120	120	120	120	23,420
IRR=36.2%						

If however, the investor were targeting an IRR in excess of 40% for an investment such as this, he would then need a greater proportion (or ownership percentage) of the year 5 terminal value. He would simply recalculate his IRR using different proportions of the terminal value until he obtained the targeted IRR (he would find that he would achieve a 40.44% IRR if he owned 35% of the terminal value).

Buy-out valuation follows the same method; the only difference is that buy-outs almost always involve debt. The amount of all debt outstanding at the terminal value date must be subtracted from the terminal value to obtain the value of company available to the equity holders. The terminal value is then allocated amongst the other providers of capital and management: mezzanine may be holding options or warrants for a certain portion of the shares, management will be entitled to another portion, and the rest is the investor's.

Determining the split of ownership and equity value is basically a process of 'trial and error', whereby differing portions of the equity value are allocated to the various providers of capital and management until everyone achieves the right returns. If the balance cannot be struck, then the deal doesn't get done.

■ Ratchets

One of the mechanisms venture capitalists have introduced to balance return objectives is the 'ratchet' in which allocation of equity varies, depending on certain pre-agreed targets or benchmarks. A performance ratchet (probably the most frequently used), specifies a higher proportion of equity (terminal value) for the management if pre-agreed corporate profit targets are exceeded. For example, the management team may initially own 25% of a company but will be able to increase their ownership share to say, 35%, on a sliding scale, based on operating earnings achieved by the company. The ratchet presupposes that higher profits will result in a higher corporate value, which would enhance the investor's IRR. Giving up part of the extra potential return to management not only provides an incentive but also may help overcome an impasse in the initial negotiations over the equity split.

Other ratchet benchmarks have included:

IRR target

If investors achieve a pre-agreed IRR on realisation of their investment, the gain above the targeted IRR would be split between the investors and the management team according to a predetermined formula.

Market capitalisation

Management may be entitled to a greater portion of the equity value if they are successful in selling or floating the company above pre-agreed targeted levels. While essentially the same as an IRR benchmark, this ratchet focuses management's attention on the fundamental objective of maximising the shareholders' return.

These ratchet targets have been criticised on the basis that IRR and market capitalisation may have more to do with stock market conditions at the time of realisation (particularly in the case of a flotation) than with the company's and management's own performance. For this reason, this type of ratchet tends to be less popular amongst venture capitalists. Others would argue that they are indifferent as to how the value was achieved; if partially, or largely through luck or timing, then so be it.

■ Structuring Buy-outs

Structuring a buy-out usually begins by determining the maximum level of debt that the target company can support. The venture capitalist, in consultation with one or more banks, can usually reach a reasonably accurate conclusion as to the amount and degree of leverage acceptable in the market for a particular transaction.

There are two basic tests of debt capacity:

1 the advance rate against assets; this gives the lender an estimate of how much collateral he has for a loan – the secondary source of repayment in the event of business failure;

2 interest cover level: buy-out lenders fundamentally concentrate on a company's ability to generate cash flow to service debt; a minimum coverage ratio (free cash flow/interest expense) of 1.5x in the initial year of the transaction, rising to 2.0x by the second year is generally necessary

(in the absence of exceptional earnings growth or cash inflows in later years) in order for the company to be able to repay the bulk of its senior debt during a seven-year term. If the collateral position is weak (if the company is in a low-asset business, for example) then the lender generally expects stronger interest coverage to compensate for the weak fallback position.

Considering these two basic criteria in the context of the company's financial forecasts, the venture capitalist and the senior lender will sketch out a debt structure. The venture capitalist will then test returns for the ordinary share capital, and then layer in other forms of debt and equity to match potential with targeted returns. The capital structure may then be adjusted during the due-diligence process to accommodate changes in assumptions.

The major differences of opinion amongst the financiers usually concern the ability of the company to achieve its financial forecasts, or whether the forecasts are realistic to begin with. The final result is as much an art as a science.

Using Discounted Cash Flow Methods to Value Companies

Discounted cash flow (DCF) methods of valuing companies have become by far the most common way of valuing companies by corporate finance advisers. Venture capitalists do not tend to use these methods as much as investment bankers, probably because they concentrate their efforts on deriving the financial projections – the free cash flows – rather than the other ingredient of the DCF method – the discount rate.

The value that venture capitalists put on their investment targets also reflects their own required rate of return, which is the discount rate they use to value future cash flows. Rather than deriving a discount rate through the Capital Asset Pricing Model, and applying this to the projected free cash flows of the company to derive a value, the venture capitalist already knows what return he is seeking and how he may be able to enhance that return through the use of lower-cost forms of capital (i.e., debt). *The amount of total capital which he can raise is the value of the business.* This, then, is the fundamental difference in approach between the corporate buyer and the financial buyer – the venture capitalist.

Exercise 4

1. Why do venture capitalists look to the future when they are trying to determine a value for a company today?

2. How does the venture capitalist determine debt capacity?

3. What purpose(s) do ratchets serve in structuring the equity component of venture capital investments?

    a) they help an investor enhance his IRR.

    b) they help the venture capitalist negotiate the split of equity between the management and himself.

    c) they provide an incentive to the management team to outperform the financial forecast.

IDEAS FOR FURTHER READING

Principles of Corporate Finance, International Edition
Brealey and Meyers: McGraw-Hill, 1988

Journal of Applied Corporate Finance
Merton Miller: '*Leverage*': Stern Stewart Management Services, Inc., Volume 4 Number 2, Summer 1991

Valuation – Measuring and Managing the Value of Companies (Second edition)
Copeland, Koller, and Murrin, (McKinsey & Co., Inc.): John Wiley & Sons, 1994

3i – Fifty Years Investing in Industry
Coopey and Clarke: Oxford University Press, 1995

Buy-outs
Quarterly Review from the Centre for Management Buy-out Research
Wright and Robbie: Management University of Nottingham, calendar quarters

GLOSSARY

Amortisation The expensing of an intangible asset over a period of time judged to be the economic life of the asset. Like depreciation, amortisation is a non-cash expense, but may be deductible for taxes.

Buy-out Generic term for the acquisition of a company in which the finance raised for the acquisition is based entirely on the assets and cash flow of the company being acquired.

CAPM Capital Asset Pricing Model, used to calculate a company's cost of equity or equivalently, an investor's required rate of return.

Common (or ordinary) share capital The shares which represent the ultimate economic ownership of a company and which almost always have voting rights.

Cost of equity The rate of return required by an investor in a company's common shares; alternatively, the rate of return a company would need to offer to existing or new common shareholders in order to raise common share capital.

Discount rate The rate used to discount future cash flows to obtain a present value.

EBIT Earnings Before Interest and Tax (often referred to as operating earnings or operating profits); represents the earnings generated by the operations or trading of the company.

EBIT multiple The value of, or price paid for, a company divided by the company's EBIT.

Earnings per share (EPS) After-tax earnings divided by the number of shares (ordinary or common) outstanding.

Free cashflow (FCF) Cashflow generated by the company's operations before deducting financing costs or discretionary expenditure. FCF represents the amount of cash available to the providers of capital. Sometimes referred to as 'operating cash flow'.

Internal rate of return (IRR) The rate at which all cash flows from an investment are discounted to give a net present value of 0 (nil); alternatively, the compounded rate of return achieved from an investment taking into consideration all cash outflows and inflows over a specified period of time.

Leveraged buy-out (LBO) A buy-out in which debt forms a significant proportion of the finance used in the transaction.

Management buy-out (MBO) A buy-out in which the existing management team of a company takes a significant or controlling stake in the company through the transaction.

Market capitalisation The total number of a company's outstanding common or ordinary shares multiplied by the market price per share.

Market premium The difference between the rate of return achieved in a public stock market and the risk-free rate of return, such as that obtained on a top-rated government security.

Market-to-book ratio A company's market capitalisation divided by its net worth.

Mezzanine finance The layer of capital which falls between senior debt and equity. Mezzanine is a sub-category of subordinated debt, usually provided by banks or mezzanine specialists in buy-out transactions.

Net present value (NPV) The discounted, current value of future cashflows generated from an investment, less the initial cost of the investment.

Net worth The difference between total assets and total liabilities shown on a company's balance sheet; sometimes referred to as 'net asset value' (NAV), 'net book value' (NBV), or simply 'book value'.

Present value (PV) The current value of future cashflow(s), derived by discounting the future cashflow(s) by a specific rate, e.g., an investor's required rate of return.

Price/earnings ratio (PER or P/E) A company's market capitalisation divided by its total net earnings. Equivalently, the market price of one share divided by EPS.

ROE Return On Equity, calculated as net earnings (after all deductions except dividends) divided by net worth of a company.

Senior debt Debt instruments which rank ahead of all other forms of capital in terms of their claim on a company's assets and cashflow.

Subordinated debt Debt which ranks behind senior debt, but ahead of preference shares and other forms of equity, in its claim on a company's cash flow and assets (in a liquidation).

Systematic risk General risks affecting all companies to some degree, e.g., political events, increases in corporate tax rate, the price of oil, etc., and which cannot be eliminated by holding a diverse portfolio of shares.

Tax shield The savings a company makes on its cost of debt due to the deductibility of interest expense from taxable income. Calculated as interest expense multiplied by the corporate tax rate.

Tangible Net Worth Net worth less all intangible assets of a company. Intangible assets include such items as: goodwill, trademarks, brand names, patents, intellectual property.

Terminal Value The value of a company at some point in the future; calculated as a multiple of earnings or through DCF method of valuing future cash flows.

Unsystematic risk Risks specific to a company, e.g. death of key executive, unexpected success of new product, etc., which can be eliminated by holding a diverse share portfolio.

Exercise 1

1. The UK is more lender-friendly from a legal standpoint. The London stock market is one of the largest in the world and a healthy stock market is critical to a buy-out market. There are also cultural differences which promote the profit motive amongst UK managers seeking to buy their businesses.

2. 3i provides about half of the early-stage capital in the UK with the rest coming from specialists, including the tax-structured Venture Capital Trusts. On the Continent, government-sponsored funding schemes provide the bulk of the capital for start-ups.

3. Buy-outs are less risky than start-ups because the companies being acquired are generally established businesses. Buy-out transactions are also larger, providing the potential for a much greater absolute return for the investor.

Exercise 2

1. A mature company experiencing slow growth, not requiring substantial investment in either fixed assets or working capital and therefore capable of producing strong and reliable cash flows.

2. b.

3. Early-stage companies pose considerable business risks, such as unproven products or markets, and therefore do not have predictable cash flows in initial years. Business risks should not be compounded with financial risk.

Exercise 3

1. It is almost always secured; has a term of up to seven years; has fairly extensive financial covenants; is priced at with lending margins of 1.5%–2.5% and upfront fees of 1%–2% of the principal amount.

2. c and d are not true.

3. They are providing the riskiest form of capital.

Exercise 4

1. Because early-stage companies have no track record and no apparent current value; most if not all of the value will be created in the future.

2. He considers the collateral coverage for the total amount of the loan and the cash flow coverage of interest and scheduled principal repayments over a normal five- to seven-year term. The amount of debt the company can support will be covered by cash flow, allowing for a margin for underperformance.

3. b and c.

ORDER FORM

Please complete and return this form to Kim Whiting, Pitman Publishing, FREEPOST, 128 Long Acre, London WC2E 9BR, UK
or fax your order on 0171 240 5771 or telephone on 0171 447 2000.

LEVEL 1 INTRODUCTION TO:	Qty	Cost
1 Corporate Credit Risk		
2 Capital Markets		
3 Treasury Management		
4 Derivatives		
5 Foreign Exchange		
6 Money Markets		
7 Futures and Options		
8 Corporate Finance		
9 Fund Management		
10 The City of London and its Institutions		
11 SWAPS		
12 Finance of Foreign Trade		
13 Documentary Credits		
14 Emerging Markets		
15 HP and Leasing Finance		
16 Back Office Settlements		
17 Financial Statements		
18 Venture Capital		
19 Mergers and Acquisitions		
20 Finance for the Non-Financial Manager		
TOTAL NUMBER OF WORKBOOKS		

All priced at £19.95 each

PAYMENT (*Please complete*)

Postage and packing:

UK: Please add £3.00 per order.

Elsewhere in Europe: Please add £5.00 for first workbook and £3.00 per book thereafter.

Rest of world: Please add £9.00 for first workbook and £6.00 per book thereafter.

☐ I enclose a cheque payable to *Pitman Publishing* for _____ (total)

☐ Please debit my Access/Visa/Barclaycard/Mastercard for _____ (total)

Card number ☐☐☐☐ ☐☐☐☐ ☐☐☐☐ ☐☐☐☐

Expiry date _____ Signature _____

Mr/Mrs/Miss/Ms   Initials _____ Surname _____

Job title _____ Department _____

Company _____

Address _____

Town _____ Country _____

Postcode _____ Telephone _____

All prices quoted are in Sterling. Value Added Tax number GB 213 6785 61. We occasionally make our customer lists available to companies whose products or services may be of interest. Anyone not wanting this free service should write 'exclude from other mailings' on this form. A Division of Pearson Professional.

Please send me details on:

☐ Levels 2 and 3 in this series

☐ Financial training programmes

☐ Other finance publications.

Customised editions of the workbooks are available. Telephone Kim Whiting at Pitman Publishing to discuss your particular needs.